MINDFUL ACTIONS

JOHN SHEARER
MINDFULNESS COACH & MENTOR

BALBOA.
PRESS
A DIVISION OF HAY HOUSE

Interior Graphics/Art Credit:
Maureen Shearer

Balboa Press books may be ordered through booksellers or by contacting:

Balboa Press
A Division of Hay House
1663 Liberty Drive
Bloomington, IN 47403
www.balboapress.com.au
1 (877) 407-4847

Because of the dynamic nature of the Internet, any web addresses or links contained in this book may have changed since publication and may no longer be valid. The views expressed in this work are solely those of the author and do not necessarily reflect the views of the publisher, and the publisher hereby disclaims any responsibility for them.

The author of this book does not dispense medical advice or prescribe the use of any technique as a form of treatment for physical, emotional, or medical problems without the advice of a physician, either directly or indirectly. The intent of the author is only to offer information of a general nature to help you in your quest for emotional and spiritual well-being. In the event you use any of the information in this book for yourself, which is your constitutional right, the author and the publisher assume no responsibility for your actions.

Any people depicted in stock imagery provided by Thinkstock are models, and such images are being used for illustrative purposes only. Certain stock imagery © Thinkstock.

Printed in the United States of America.

ISBN: 978-1-4525-2563-1 (sc)
ISBN: 978-1-4525-2564-8 (e)

Balboa Press rev. date: 09/09/2014

CONTENTS

Introduction

Gooday! ~ I have been on an amazing journey. On 9th June, 1982, I died in a truck smash and was brought back. I believed there was a reason and wanted answers. Despite extensive study into World History, Cultures and Religions, all I got was depression and addictions.

My life fell apart, not so much because of physical injuries, but because of the fifteen years of ups and downs and mental suffering that followed. I was ashamed that I had a mental disorder and refused to talk about it or get help.

That is the motivation behind my desire to help people go from meds to mindfulness. It is also the reason I am so passionate about raising awareness of both the healing and the transformational powers of mindfulness in all aspects of life.

In 1986, I completed my first course in counselling with the Smith Family. I had found my calling and completed Front Wheel Counselling in 1990 and Youth Counselling in 1996. However, I was still struggling with my thoughts and feelings. Relationships with my loved ones were also adversely affected. By 1997, I was at rock bottom. Authorities told me that my condition was incurable and I would have to take medications for the rest of my life.

That was when I got my miracle. On October 10th, 1997, a friend knocked on my door, told me his story and pointed me in the right direction. Two days later I had a Spiritual Awakening and my life slowly began to change. No more depression!

I started working again and my childhood dreams came true when my wife and I opened a Cue Sport Centre in 2003. I travelled with the Australian 8-Ball Team to Las Vegas in 2005 and performed exceptionally well. In the 2007 Australian Junior 9-Ball Championships, four of my junior players filled the semi-finals and I was dubbed Super Coach. I have no doubt this was due to the mind skills that I taught those young champions.

I still had occasional mental attacks but they were easily defeated. I was living my dream and life was good! In 2008, I lost a close friend to an asthma attack. My wife was using the same sort of breathing machine for her asthma, so we made the decision to move north to a warmer climate.

I decided to go back to counselling and began surfing the net to find out the latest and most successful therapies in the world for anxiety and depression etc. What I found was a book called 'The Happiness Trap' by Dr Russ Harris. I was sold on mindfulness and began my personal mindful practice. I have been studying the many aspects of mindfulness unceasingly ever since.

In 2009, I trained as an ACT Therapist (Acceptance & Commitment Therapy) with Dr Russ, closed the 'pool hall' in Wagga Wagga and moved to Grafton NSW. I am happy to report that my wife is pretty much free of asthma!

I accepted part-time work as a Youth Mentor with Juvenile Justice and also began coaching. I made the decision to be a Coach, because to my way of thinking, counselling infers that something is wrong with people. The truth is...people are just 'Stuck!'

Today, I am at peace with the world and live in spiritual bliss. The practice of being mindful is what got me there. My hope is for your journey to arrive at the same destination. The purpose of writing Mindful Actions is to help you along the way.

I encourage you to dream, discover your purpose and live a mindful life. You too, will experience the necessary mind shift that allows a deep connection with yourself and everyone around you. Life doesn't get better by chance...it gets better by change!

WHAT IS MINDFULNESS?

I was truly inspired by Dr Russ Harris! This is his definition of mindfulness…I have found none better!

"Mindfulness can be defined in a variety of different ways, but they all basically come down to this: Mindfulness is a transformative mental state of awareness which involves focusing your attention with flexibility, openness, and curiosity. This simple definition tells us three important things. First, mindfulness is a process of awareness, not thinking. It involves paying attention to your experience in that moment as opposed to being caught up in thoughts. In a mindful state, you can let difficult thoughts and feelings freely flow through you, without getting caught up in them or pushed around by them, and without getting into a struggle with them. Second, mindfulness involves a particular attitude: one of openness and curiosity. Even if our experience in the moment is difficult, painful or unpleasant, we can be open to and curious about it instead of running from, fighting with or trying to avoid it. Third, mindfulness involves flexibility of attention: the ability to consciously direct, broaden or focus attention on different aspects of experience. We can use mindfulness to 'wake up,' connect with ourselves and appreciate the fullness of each moment of life. We can use it to improve our self-knowledge – to learn more about how we feel, think and react. We can use it to connect deeply and intimately with the people we care about, including ourselves. And we can use it to consciously influence our own behaviour and increase our range of responses to the world we inhabit. It is the actions of living consciously – a profound way to enhance psychological resilience and increase life satisfaction."

Thank you Dr Russ Harris.

WHAT ARE THE BENEFITS?

A good friend is hard to find, hard to lose and impossible to forget! The best way to have a friend - is to be a friend. Give your friend a copy of *Mindful Actions*, spend time together, and talk about the benefits of practicing mindfulness.

Mindfulness can help you to:

- develop self-acceptance and self-compassion
- rise above fear, doubt and insecurity
- build genuine confidence
- reduce stress and worry
- handle painful thoughts and feelings effectively
- break self-defeating habits
- develop a resilient mindset
- improve performance in music and sport
- build good memory function for study
- find fulfilment in your work
- build deeper and more satisfying relationships
- create a rich, full and meaningful life

Stay in touch with your friend and encourage each other to practice being mindful. It is my hope that your friend happens to be your best friend or life partner. I have witnessed couples going in different directions when only one has chosen the road to enlightenment. This is very understandable when you consider the life-changing effects of such a journey.

Of course, you may choose to embark on this journey alone. I have created this "coaching manual" to be a guide on that journey. I recommend that you read one mindful action every three to seven days and then practise that action. It will take three to six months of mindful practice to be well and truly on your way to living a mindful life - a life full of love, peace and happiness.

HAPPINESS

Having a mindful practice makes happiness an automatic choice. Happiness is a bi-product of mindfulness. Happiness isn't a destination, it's the journey! This mindful action is to wake up every day with a determination to be happy. Don't let anything or anybody steal your happiness.

Do you remember the last really good belly laugh you had, and how good it felt? Clearly, the antidote for a fast and serious lifestyle is to have a good laugh. Did you know that you can fake a good laugh? Those lucky enough to be with you will start laughing as well. Try it! Happiness is a choice! Here is a collection of my favourite happiness quotes to help put it into perspective:

- "Happiness does not depend on what you have or who you are. It solely relies on what you think." [Buddha]
- "Happiness is like a butterfly. The more you chase it, the more it eludes you. But if you turn your attention to other things, it comes and sits softly on your shoulder." [Henry David Thoreau]

- "Happiness is when what you think, what you say, and what you do are in harmony" [Mahatma Gandhi]
- "It isn't what you have, or who you are, or where you are, or what you are doing that makes you happy or unhappy. It is what you think about." [Dale Carnegie]
- "The more we care for the happiness of others, the greater is our own sense of well being." [Dalai Lama]
- "I, not events, have the power to make me happy or unhappy today. I can choose which it shall be. Yesterday is dead, tomorrow hasn't arrived yet. I have just one day, today, and I'm going to be happy in it." [Groucho Marx]
- "The primary cause of unhappiness is never the situation but your thoughts about it." ~ Eckhart Tolle
- "Most folks are about as happy as they make their minds up to be." [Abraham Lincoln]
- "For every minute you are angry you lose sixty seconds of happiness." [Ralph Waldo Emerson]
- "There is no way to happiness - happiness is the way." [Dr Wayne W Dyer]

BE MINDFUL!

Aristotle said, "The energy of the mind is the essence of life". People suffer with painful thoughts and feelings because they feel 'stuck.' They are often diagnosed with an illness that makes them feel even more stuck. Mindfulness is a simple yet powerful way to get 'unstuck'. Mindfulness is a discipline of the mind which requires practise! The result of your efforts is peace of mind and real freedom from your thoughts!

As mindfulness coach, I encourage you to make your key thought from this moment - and into the future - *'Be Mindful'* This mindful action is to use *'Be Mindful'* whenever you have an unhelpful thought or feeling. Anytime you find yourself in a stressful situation or under pressure, let *'Be Mindful'* be the trigger to take you to a place of peaceful presence or of heightened awareness.

Being mindful is the ongoing practice of pausing your mind chatter and focusing your attention on the present moment with awareness. Our minds are like radio stations, broadcasting 24/7. Quieting your thoughts doesn't come naturally so I will say once again, you will need to practice! Nothing is worth more than this moment; in fact, it's all you will ever have!

A great way to get the feel of mindfulness is to still your mind and listen intently. Pick a relatively quiet time and be totally aware of your immediate surroundings. Name five things you can hear. Notice how the rest of the world doesn't exist in those moments of concentration. You will be amazed how things prioritise themselves. This is a practical example of being mindful. You can be mindful at any time throughout the day.

'Be Mindful' Say it five times if you have to. Say it to yourself when you are distracted with negativity, worry or anxiety. Practise this once or twice daily to start and then increase until it becomes habit. Slow down - *'Be Mindful'*

YOU ARE NOT YOUR THOUGHTS!

Lao Tzu said, "Silence is a source of great strength" Thinking too much can only cause problems. Left to itself the mind wanders through all kinds of thoughts; including thoughts expressing anger, self-pity, revenge, depression, and anxiety. As you indulge in these kinds of thoughts and feelings, you reinforce emotions in your heart and cause yourself to suffer. What can we do about this?

'You are *not* your thoughts.' The first time I heard somebody say that, I didn't like the sound of it at all. What else could I be? I believed that the mental chatter in my head was just *'me'*, the place where all the experiences of my life happened. I can see clearly now that life is nothing but passing experiences. My thoughts are just one more category of things that I experience. Thoughts are no more fundamental than sights, sounds, and smells. Like any experience, they arise in my awareness, and then I have a choice of what to do with them. If I can observe my thoughts, just like I can observe other objects, who's doing the observing?

As mindfulness coach, this is one aspect of being mindful that is not negotiable. You need to understand this truth, or there is no point going any further. You are *not* your thoughts! This mindful action is to be the silent observer of your thoughts and feelings. The silent observer is that part of you which has been observing from the day you were born. It is the part of you that is attached to your heart and also attached to whatever you call the universe.

I encourage you to put this to the test. When an unhelpful thought comes along, *be mindful* and think *'I'm having the thought that...'* or *'thank you mind for that thought but I prefer to...'* Keep practising this and gradually, all negativity will be replaced with positivity. What you are in fact doing, is re-training your mind.

Search your heart about your silent observer. You will know this is truth. You will know the silent observer is your authentic self and is well connected. We are All One. One with Spirit. One with Life! *Be Mindful* - and Observe Your Thoughts!

AWARENESS

James Thurber said, "Let us not look back in anger, nor forward in fear, but around in awareness."

Mindfulness is being aware of what is happening in the present moment. It really is that simple!

The key is to look at your thoughts for what they really are - just thoughts. There is no need to dwell on them, act on them, fight with them or try to avoid them. Become aware of your silent observer watching your thoughts.

Your silent observer is that part of you that is pure awareness. Let's try a little mindful action using your silent observer. Sit in a comfortable position so you can be nicely relaxed. Close your eyes and focus on your five senses. Wiggle your toes and fingers to be aware of your sense of touch. Then think about your favourite aroma. Notice how you can almost smell your favourite aroma. Then think about your favourite food. Notice how you can almost taste your favourite food. Then visualise your favourite place. Notice how you can see your favourite place even though your eyes are closed. Then be aware of your surroundings by listening intently.

When you have focused on your five senses one at a time, pause your mind and notice how you can focus on all of them at once. That sense of awareness you experience is your silent observer at work. It is a process, not a thing; some call it your sixth sense.

The more you use your silent observer in your daily walk, the more you will get out of life. When your mind is going at a hundred miles an hour, life is just passing you by.

The silent observer is connected to your heart. The silent observer is also connected to both the Divine and all living things. I invite you to put this to the test. Mindfully work out what is on your heart. Put it out there in the universe; be patient and aware. It is important to be out there in the world, so that things can happen. If you're not working, be a volunteer. Always be aware of the infinite possibilities of the present moment. *Be Mindful* - and Aware!

OPEN MIND

This mindful action is especially helpful for addressing anger issues. We are all familiar with that feeling when anger is raising its ugly head. When you notice that feeling, use your key thought; *'Be Mindful'* and pause your mind with awareness. Be your silent observer and take control of the situation. You will need to be strong!

Now let's look at the other side of anger. Anger can be a useful emotion in certain situations, usually life events. I remember a time after I smashed up, when I went to the top of a hill and let it rip at the top of my voice. I was angry at the world and it felt good. My wife did the same thing after she lost her first husband in a motorcycle accident. She found it to be an excellent stress reliever!

Minds are like parachutes - they only function when open! Anger happens when the mind is closed, in other words, when the mind is made up. Be open to absolutely everything. The world is full of possibilities. You always have the choice of taking things on board or letting them go.

Don't get angry - ask questions! Be open and *respond* to situations rather than reacting. Respond with *'That's an interesting point of view, tell me more.'* or *'Would you like to hear what I think?'* Work it out, don't get worked up! Mindfully pausing your mind for five or ten seconds can make a huge difference in most situations.

An open mind goes hand in hand with an open heart. Having your heart and mind open enables thoughts from the 'source' to enter. A closed mind is not only closed to the outside world, it is often closed to itself as well. But if you can open the door, maybe just a crack to start with, the creative ideas that have been patiently waiting, will come flooding in. *Be Mindful* - and Open!

BELIEFS

1982-1997 ~ I believed that I had an imbalance of chemicals in my brain. I believed I was mentally ill and would never be cured. I believed that I would have to take medications for the rest of my life. Professional people told me these things. People who had studied and been trained for many years in Universities.

1997-2009 ~ I had a spiritual awakening and believed in the power of Spirit. No more depression and no more meds. I believed the mind was like the moon. The moon has a light side as well as a dark side. For the first time in my life, everything made sense to me. All through history I could see the evidence of this spiritual game of chess. Love, joy and peace on one side versus hate, sadness and war on the other. Minds consumed by the light, dreaming, creating and full of life versus minds consumed by the darkside, nightmarish, destroying and suicidal.

2009-2013 ~ I started the study and practice of mindfulness. I felt driven and spent countless hours in front of the computer. 20-30 hours per week, it almost drove my wife insane. Mindfulness is all about awareness and being fully connected to spirit. It is the tool we all need to live a life of peace and happiness.

2013-End of Days ~ Osho said, "It's not a question of learning much - on the contrary. It's a question of unlearning much." We all have beliefs based on what we have learned and what we have experienced. This in turn becomes our truth and we all have different truths.

The mind is like a computer and needs to be reset now and then. I decided to un-believe everything I had learned on my life's journey. As thoughts came to mind, I used my silent observer (my heart) to test for truth. The results have been absolutely enlightening! This is your mindful action. Be warned; your mind is going to object strongly, just remember, you are not your mind!

Here are a few random thoughts:

- What you believe has more power than what you dream or wish or hope for.
- You become what you believe.
- Don't believe everything you think.
- The reason you do the things you do is because you think the things you think.
- The reason you think the things you think is because you believe the things you believe.
- The root cause of your problems is not what you are doing - it is what you are thinking!

- The worst thing you can do is believe that you don't have a choice.
- Life presents you with endless choices and opportunities if you care to step out and face your fears without limiting beliefs.
- Only you can take the impossible and make it possible! *Be Mindful* - and Open to All Possibilities!

Mindful Practice

Thich Nhat Hanh said, "In practising mindfulness, we become a peaceful refuge for ourselves and others. When the seed of mindfulness in us is watered, it can grow into enlightenment, understanding, compassion, and transformation. The more we practise mindfulness, the stronger this seed will grow."

Mindfulness practice involves deliberately over-riding the tendency of your mind to go to the past or the future. It is the mindful action of repeatedly re-directing awareness to the present moment.

The hardest thing to do when you first begin your mindful practice, is remembering to practise. A little action that I started doing in the early days was to use the golden arches at McDonalds restaurants as a key to *Be Mindful!* I still do it! I am usually driving or riding my motorcycle when I see the big 'M' (M for Mindfulness) Try it!

Mindful travelling creates an excellent opportunity to practise. It doesn't matter what mode of transport you use.

You can practise when using public transport or when you are riding your bicycle. Walking is arguably the best time for mindful practice on the go.

Daily mundane chores also create an opportunity for mindful practice. Doing the dishes, cleaning the house or when brushing your teeth - when your mind wanders, and it surely will, then bring it back to the task at hand. It's not as simple as it sounds but just keep trying, it gets easier!

You know the luxurious feeling when you first get in the shower, when the water is running through your hair and over your body. You are in the moment, but then the mind takes over and before you know it, you are just going through the motions. Thinking about the list of things that need doing, or might happen, or what might have been, or what if..etc..etc.. Practise mindful awareness for the entire shower, from start to finish. Not only will you get the most out of your shower but you will start to get the most out of your life!

The following is a mindful action from Russ Harris:

"Now here's one especially useful, ultra-brief, and very simple mindfulness practice, that you can easily incorporate into your busy daily routine, no matter how pressed for time you are. It's called the Mindful S.T.O.P. Here's how it goes:

> **S** – Slow down (slow down your breathing; or slowly press your feet into the floor; or slowly

stretch your arms; or slowly press your fingertips together)

T - Take note (with a sense of curiosity, notice your thoughts & feelings; notice what you can see and hear and touch and taste and smell; notice where you are and what you are doing)

O - Open up (open up and make room for your thoughts & feelings, and allow them to freely flow through you; use any defusion or expansion skill you like)

P - Pursue values (reconnect with your values, and let them guide whatever you do next)

The lovely thing about a Mindful STOP is you can make it as short or as long as you like. You can zip through this in under thirty seconds – e.g. while you're waiting at a red traffic light, or stuck in a supermarket queue, or waiting for your kids to come sit at the dinner table – or you can stretch it out into a thirty minute formal meditation practice. I encourage you to try it out for yourself – not just once, but over and over and over again: Slow down; Take note; Open up; and Pursue your values. A regular Mindful STOP works wonders."

Russ Harris uses a couple of references to ACT (Acceptance & Commitment Therapy) in the Mindful STOP. I will be covering a little more ACT as we progress. The Mindful

STOP could also be used as a trigger to give your mind instructions, like *Be Mindful!* The whole point of the exercise is practise, practise and practise some more! It is so worth it! *Be Mindful!*

Notice with Curiosity

When my Father was on his deathbed he said "John... you're nothing but a big kid!" I looked at him for what seemed like ages and then he said "And so am I!" My children called him Inspector Gadget because he was always inventing gadgets to make life a little easier. He looked at the world around him with curiosity, always looking for ways to improve it.

There's a couple of things to learn from this when starting your mindful practice. Learn with a childlike mindset and notice your experience with curiosity. Think about children playing and how they are naturally in a mindful state. They laugh and play and 'live in the flow'. They are curious and ask lots of questions. They are creative and find solutions easily. Curiosity goes hand in hand with creativity; let's take a leaf out of their book. Life is not about finding yourself - it's about creating yourself.

Mindful awareness is about noticing the experience you are having, whether it is a thought, a feeling, what you are doing or your immediate surroundings. Everything starts with a thought.

This mindful action is to notice your thought with curiosity. Ask yourself two questions:

1. Where did the thought come from? Many in this world try to deny the darkness within, wanting only to show the light to the world. But to find true peace of the Spirit, you must embrace both the Light and the Darkside. Both sides are the key to who you are.

2. Is the thought helpful? If the answer is 'yes', then accept it, expand on it with creativity and put it into action. If the answer is 'no', then accept it and let it go! If you dwell on unhelpful thoughts, you give them power. If you fight with unhelpful thoughts, you will get stressed. If you try to avoid unhelpful thoughts, you will probably end up with addictions.

The key here is acceptance of your thoughts, good or bad. That way, you can 'live in the flow'! *Be Mindful!*

ATTENTION

Henry David Thoreau said, "As a single footstep will not make a path on the earth, so a single thought will not make a pathway in the mind. To make a deep physical path, we walk again and again. To make a deep mental path, we must think over and over the kind of thoughts we wish to dominate our lives."

We have the freedom to choose what we give our attention to and what we believe about ourselves, our situation, others and life in general. This is a huge responsibility, as it determines to a great extent what our experience of life will be. Be mindful of your choices, especially when you feel stressed.

When you feel stressed or under pressure with a lot going on around you, try this mindful action. Take a deep breath and as you slowly breathe out, try to empty your mind and focus on your surroundings. Take a second breath if you have to, this action only takes 10-20 seconds. Give your undivided attention to the present moment with heightened awareness of what is going on around you. Take notice what comes to mind first - this most often helps determine your priority. Try it!

Here's a mindful action worth giving attention to - taking mindful bites. Have you ever eaten an entire meal and not tasted a single bite? Next time you eat, bring all your senses with you and experience each bite from start to finish. It's not as easy as it sounds, stay present and be amazed by the simple things in life.

Has one of your loved ones ever asked 'have you been listening to me?" or "did you hear what I just said?" The greatest gift you can give the people you love is your attention. The mindful action of engaging with total presence, will deepen your relationships. If the love in your life has been waning a little, practice less mind and more heart. *Be Mindful* in Love!

JUDGEMENTS

Ram Dass said, "The heart surrenders everything to the moment. The mind judges and holds back."

Be Mindful and replace judgements with curiosity. When you notice your mind making a judgement, pause and redirect your focus with curiosity. Your outer world will be a much more interesting place and your inner world will be more peaceful. People who judge don't matter - people who matter, don't judge!

"I'm not good enough" "What's the use?" "I can't do this anymore" "I'm too fat" "I'm not smart enough" are examples of self judgements. When a self judgement comes to mind, be mindful and become your silent observer for a moment. Remind yourself that you are not your thoughts and redirect your focus to your values or purpose.

The silent observer doesn't judge. Any sort of judgement is wasting time and energy. Judgements are a distraction away from your authentic self. The silent observer is the connection between the Divine and all other life on earth.

It is that connection with the Light that allows you to see the light in yourself and see the light in others. Namaste.

The mindful action of being non-judgemental is not easy because it goes against human nature. Take a look at history or what's currently happening both in the world, and in the world around you. You will see the results of people passing judgement on each other. You will see the division, the hatred and the fighting.

When you notice your mind passing judgement; stop, be mindful and refocus with curiosity. Then try understanding, acceptance and love; both on yourself and others. The results will be increased self-esteem and compassion. You may find yourself building bridges and making new friends. You may also find yourself changing others and changing yourself. *Be Mindful!*

LETTING GO

Ajahn Chah said, "Do everything with a mind that lets go. If you let go a little you a will have a little peace; if you let go a lot you will have a lot of peace; if you let go completely you will have complete peace."

This mindful action is to get into the habit of letting go. I love the way that Paulo Coelho pulls no punches when he said, "That is why it is so important to let certain things go. To release them. To cut loose. People need to understand that no one is playing marked cards; sometimes we win and sometimes we lose. Don't expect to get anything back, don't expect recognition for your efforts, don't expect your genius to be discovered or your love to be understood. Complete the circle. Not out of pride, inability, or arrogance but simply because whatever it is, it no longer fits in your life. Close the door, change the record, clean the house, get rid of the dust. Stop being who you were and become who you are."

We all face challenges, heartache and tragedies that make us think: "how can this be good?" or "I will never get over it!" It is okay to be angry or upset at first. Getting over a painful experience is much like crossing monkey bars. You have to let go at some point in order to move forward.

If a painful thought keeps coming back, make room for it, rather than dwelling on it, trying to avoid it or fighting with it. What you resist, persists! Making room for it is the best way to let it go. That may not make sense at first. Be mindful and use the silent observer for a moment. Notice you are having the thought and say "thank you mind for that thought" or "Clever mind! You do come up with some good ones!" Then shift your focus to a value. More about working out your values later.

If the thought has ballooned into a painful story, then give the story a name. That way, when the story comes to mind, you can say; Ahh! Here's the old "Why me?" story or the "Not good enough" story or "What's the point?" story. Then make room for it by playing mind games. Be creative and imagine the "whatever" story in the circus performing some act or on the big screen as an illuminated sign or on a stage performing a song and dance.

Knowledge is learning something every day. Wisdom is letting go of something every day. *Be Mindful!*

ACCEPTANCE

Thich Nhat Hanh said, "To be beautiful means to be yourself. You don't need to be accepted by others. You need to accept yourself."

Why compare yourself with others? No one in the whole wide world can do a better job of being you, than you.

Be Mindful in the way you experience negative emotions. True mindfulness accepts the good and the bad equally. Next time you feel upset or sick, be kind to yourself and fully accept it as your present mental or physical condition.

This mindful action is choosing to adopt an open, curious and accepting attitude with your experience. Use your silent observer with thoughts, emotions, urges and memories as they arise, even when they are unpleasant. Make a pact with yourself to validate, accept and love who you are. Even the yucky bits you'd like to change.

When you accept yourself the way you are right now, new possibilities in your life begin to surface. No longer will you have the fear of what people think. I believe the fear of what people think is the biggest fear in the world today. It stops multitudes of people from taking that first step on their road to fulfilling their purpose.

Accepting where you are right now in your journey leaves your mind open to new opportunities. When you struggle or try to get rid of mental or physical pain, you are closing down your mind and life will pass you by. Acceptance is a choice. *Be Mindful!*

FOCUS ON VALUES

Dr. Wayne Dyer said, "If you change the way you look at things, the things you look at change".

Be proactive in your thought life because *You* need to take care of *You*. Make decisions that are based on your personal values. When painful or negative thoughts show up, be mindful and shift your focus to your values. What are your values? Values are different to goals. Goals are about ticking boxes when you achieve them. Values are an ongoing process where the boxes never get ticked.

One way of working out your values is to imagine yourself at your own funeral. Then imagine what you would like your loved ones to be saying about you. When I first did this exercise, I imagined my kids saying "Dad always had time for me". Then I made a decision to take them to the river that weekend. I got proactive in my physical life as well as my thought life.

Another exercise you can do is to imagine you are at your 40th, 60th or 80th birthday party. Three people give speeches about what you stand for and what you mean to them. Once again, imagine what you would most like them to be saying about you. Here is a list of some of the areas they might cover:

- Friendship
- Intimate Relationship
- Family and Parenting
- Employment
- Culture
- Health and Spirituality
- Creativity and Passion
- Nature and Environment
- Sport and Activities
- Education and Learning
- Exploration and Travel

Working out your values is important because it enables the mindful action of shifting your focus from negative to positive. It is also very helpful to be mindful of your values when you are working out your goals. What is most important is to then make a commitment to take positive action based on those values! *Be Mindful!*

COMMITMENT

None of us come from an ideal family. There's a good chance that you may have to overcome your upbringing. Many of you have experienced things like poverty; physical, emotional, verbal or sexual abuse; rejection; drug addiction; alcoholism; rage; divorce etc.

Years later you are still struggling with things like low self-esteem, loneliness, relationship failure, addiction, overeating, depression, anxiety, anger issues or stress related problems.

Here's the thing - having a bad start doesn't mean you can't have a great finish. Your life today is not about what happened yesterday, it's about what you do with what happened yesterday. Think of your background as lessons learned and make your history a foundation for your purpose. When unhelpful thoughts or feelings pop up from the past, focus on your values and take committed action.

It is commitment to take values guided action that will get you on track to having a life worth living. It is commitment to make the necessary changes in your thinking to enable a mind shift to take place. It is commitment to start or continue practising mindfulness on a daily basis that will open your world to infinite possibilities.

This mindful action is to make that commitment right now. Commit to five minutes of practising mindful awareness first thing in the morning and five minutes last thing at night. Commit to using your key thought *Be Mindful!* which triggers twenty to thirty seconds of pausing your mind with awareness. Commit to doing this at least twice a day or anytime it is needed throughout your day.

Whatever you are struggling with - *Be Mindful!*

ACTION

Actions turn what's possible into reality. You can't just think your way out of a difficult situation. No matter how positive and focused you are on what you want in life, you still need to take action. Some people are 90% inspiration and 10% perspiration; what they really need is 10% inspiration and 90% perspiration!

This is especially common amongst people with drug and alcohol addictions. They get high and full of world changing ideas. They feel inspired and happy with their creativity. Next morning they return to earth, feeling a little flat so they start planning another hit. Of course, you don't need to be on drugs to live that kind of life.

Do you feel like your life is going around in circles, like being stuck on a merry-go-round? Put your energy into taking action that is based on your values and the things you are passionate about. It is important to have a dream that is based on your purpose. It is also important to visualise where you would like your life to be down the track a bit. Then work towards your vision with mindful purpose.

The way to creating change in your life is by doing one small thing today that is different than it was yesterday. What you do today is what you will have tomorrow. Make your tomorrow better by taking action today. We have all heard the saying; actions speak louder than words!

Whenever you find yourself a bit down, stressed or overwhelmed; try this mindful action. Ask yourself these two questions - it's a great way to get your mind and life back on track!

1. What's the No.1 thing I could start doing today that, if I did it consistently, would have the most positive impact in my life? ~ Then just do it!
2. What's the No.1 thing I could stop doing right now, that if I stopped doing it, would have the greatest positive impact in my life? ~ Then stop doing it!

I never said practising mindfulness was easy. I said being mindful is simple. If you aren't happy with your life because of addictions; take mindful action! Let's say for example, you are a smoker. Each time you light up, have a mindful look at whatever you are smoking. Look at what you are doing with mindful awareness for twenty seconds. Take notice what comes to your mind. Your authentic self will eventually come through and you will take action. You can do the same with food if you aren't happy with your weight. *Be Mindful!*

LISTENING

Jimi Hendrix said, "Knowledge speaks but wisdom listens."

The word 'listen' contains the same letters as the word 'silent'. What can you hear right now? Stop thinking for twenty to thirty seconds and be mindful by listening. Listen so intently that you become aware of awareness itself. Take notice of this peaceful experience.

When you communicate mindfully with another person, you are making a commitment to really hear what the person is saying. Wait patiently for your turn to speak and concentrate to the max. When you notice your thoughts drifting off, and they *will* try; become your silent observer by coming back to the present moment.

Bringing awareness to listening improves empathy and compassion and will improve relationships beyond belief! Can you listen without agreeing or disagreeing, liking or disliking or planning what you will say next? This mindful action takes a lot of practice.

Try listening with awareness when you meet people. You will be amazed how well you remember their names. Remembering names is the most valuable asset in business relationships as well as personal. Try to be mindfully aware when you are listening to the teacher, lecturer, presenter or coach. When you are fully present, your silent observer doesn't miss a thing and you will be able to trust your memory. Total recall is the most valuable asset in exams, assignments, reporting and conversations.

Whenever you hear a phone ring, a bird sing, a train pass, laughter, a car horn, the wind, or the sound of a door closing – use any sound as a prompt to be mindful and stop thinking. Listen to be fully present and fully awake. Life will never pass you by when you are using your key - *Be Mindful!*

Listen - do you hear birds singing? Put on some music today that just beckons you to break out in song; the birds do it, why can't you? Nothing quite like a good old favourite song to make your day joyful and happy - Right?

Forgiveness

Dr Martin Luther King Jnr said, "Forgiveness is not an occasional act, it is a constant attitude."

Forgiveness is a gift - a gift that you give yourself! It is a mindful choice that gives peace of mind in the present moment. Forgiveness changes the memory of your past into a hope for your future.

This mindful action is to stop holding on to the past. It is to release regrets about whatever you failed to do or might have done that didn't go well. It is to forgive others for whatever they failed to do or might have done that harmed you in some way. Make a mindful declaration today to make a new beginning.

Let go of the past and move on. Your mind may be thinking "that's easy to say!" or "I've tried that but it doesn't work!" Remember, you are not your thoughts, be mindful by connecting with your silent observer.

Find time to go to your favourite place of nature for a bit of solitude. Think about the things you think you can't let go, then quieten your mind and use all your senses to become mindfully aware of your surroundings. Make a deep connection by listening, first to nature and then to your heart.

Notice your sense of peace and sense of knowing in those mindful moments. When you rejoin the rat race, you will be able to recall those moments when your past tries to haunt you. Recall, be mindful and shift your focus to your values. Take values guided action and create a joyful new future for yourself.

Here's some news from the establishment. Researchers have recently become interested in studying the effects of forgiveness. Evidence is mounting that holding on to grudges and bitterness results in long-term health problems. Forgiveness, on the other hand, offers numerous benefits, including:

- Lower blood pressure
- Stress reduction
- Less hostility
- Better anger management skills
- Lower heart rate
- Lower risk of alcohol or substance abuse
- Fewer depression symptoms
- Fewer anxiety symptoms
- Reduction in chronic pain

- More friendships
- Healthier relationships
- Greater religious or spiritual well-being
- Improved psychological well-being

Unforgiveness is like drinking poison and expecting the other person to die! Forgiveness really isn't about the other person at all. Forgiveness is the choice you make to be kind and loving to yourself. It then has a flow on effect to your loved ones and the people you care about. *Be Mindful* and Forgive!

GRATITUDE

Henry David Thoreau said, "I am grateful for what I am and have. My thanksgiving is perpetual. It is surprising how contented one can be with just a sense of existence."

Your perception of the world changes as you become mindfully aware of gratitude. As your gratitude increases, so does your happiness! Why? Because gratitude helps make sense of your past, brings peace for the present moment and creates a vision for the future. It is gratitude that enables you to receive with acceptance. It is gratitude that motivates you to repay the goodness that you have been given, by giving to others. It is gratitude that enables you to be fully human.

Gratitude and happiness are intertwined, because when you feel thankful for what you have, you can't help but be cheerful. You can increase your gratitude and happiness simply by bringing images to mind that give you a sense of joy.

In addition to that mindful action, take a look around you and notice what's positive, beautiful and wonderful in your life. Take a moment right now to observe your surroundings and find things that are beautiful or wondrous.

Just sit quietly and allow 'bliss' to rise within you. Focus on gratitude, things you value and people you love. *Be Mindful!*

ATTITUDE

This mindful action is to adopt an attitude that will be of service, both to yourself and those you care about. Life is short, don't waste time worrying about what people might be thinking about you. The truth is - they probably aren't thinking anything at all! Life is too short to wake up with regrets.

Believe everything happens for a reason. If you get a second chance, grab it with both hands. If it changes your life, let it be. Do not continue to live in the same old way. Make up your mind to do something to improve your life, and then take action!

Nothing is real to you unless you make it real. Nothing can touch you unless you let it touch you. Think positive thoughts and really believe in yourself. Wake up with a determination to be happy - no matter what!

Almost always, you have a choice as to what attitude to adopt. There is nothing in any normal situation that dictates you must react one way or another. As a matter of fact, don't react at all - *Be mindful* and respond!

If you feel angry about something that happens, for instance, that's how you choose to feel. Nothing in the incident itself makes it absolutely necessary for you to feel that way. It is your choice. And since you do have a choice, most of the time you'll be better off if you choose to respond in a positive rather than a negative way. Once you replace negative thoughts with positive ones, you'll start having positive results.

Any circumstance you find yourself in is only temporary and can change in an instant. Your attitude and mindful state is the steering wheel of your life, what you think about and project into a situation intensifies and eventually manifests in real life. Meet every circumstance with a positive outlook and when setbacks come - hold your course! The dawn will break! *Be Mindful!*

CONNECT

This mindful action is to practise connecting fully with the Divine and all life on earth. The best time is when you come out of your dream-state. This could be when you wake up or anytime you use your trigger *Be Mindful!* and become your silent observer. In those moments when you quieten your mind, practice using all your senses to connect with whatever you call the universe as well as the world around you.

Ted Murray reached great heights in the tennis coaching world using mindfulness. This is what he said recently:

"Trust in the synchronicity of the universe. When you begin to open up to the idea that your intention attracts the right people and circumstances into your life, then it truly seems like magic happens. You create abundance in ways that go way beyond money. You receive guidance from sources that couldn't possibly have randomly crossed your path. You meet just the right person to partner with or to help each other grow through the most unlikely of circumstances. Instead of seeing these things as unrelated random acts and that you just happen to be lucky, see the entire realm of possibilities you can experience. All it takes is a strong desire and a focused intention on what you want to create. If it is for the benefit of all and not just a selfish desire, then the universe will conspire to help you. It doesn't require a detailed road map. A clear focus on the destination is all that is needed. Let the universe create the most delightful and unexpected path to get there that will be far more adventurous and amazing than your mind could ever imagine. Use your mind to visualize, then just follow your heart and see what magical places your path might lead."

Many thanks to Ted Murray for his mindful wisdom. True connection is a process, not a quick fix or miracle cure. You will need to practice unceasingly and have great patience.

It took me four years, and looking back, I liken the whole process to that of an apprenticeship. There are many lessons to learn, and as you become more aware, you start to notice the ingenious ways that the Divine synchronises your life.

Start slow and take small steps. Isolation is the enemy. It is very important to get out there and connect with the world. Focus on feeling the connection with good eye contact and mindful listening. Be curious and look for deeper meaning in what people say. Train your mind to be more and more present, without judgement. Live in the flow and let life come to you. *Be Mindful!*

DREAM

Here are three of my favourite quotes to encourage you to dream. The best dreams are the ones you have while you are awake. Don't dream about money or possessions. Once you have got to know yourself fairly well, you will know what your values are and also the thing you are most passionate about. As you dream, keep your focus on values and passion.

- "Imagination is everything. It is the preview of life's coming attractions." [Albert Einstein]
- "You can't just sit there and wait for people to give you that golden dream, you've got to get out there and make it happen for yourself." [Diana Ross]
- "Twenty years from now you will be more disappointed by the things you didn't do than by the things you did. So throw off the bowlines. Sail away from the safe harbour... Explore. Dream." [Mark Twain]

Life without hopes and dreams is like riding a bike with no destination. Take all that you've become, to be all that you can be. This mindful action is to create the life of your dreams! It may take awhile so take the first step today. I am sure you have heard the saying from Lao Tzu "A journey of a thousand miles begins with a single step" Life's short! Live your dream and share your passion! *Be Mindful!*

PURPOSE

Mark Twain said, "The two most important days of your life are the day you are born, and the day you find out why."

Are you running on automatic pilot? Just going through the motions? Even worse; do you feel like you are on a merry-go-round and can't get off? It is so easy to get all caught up in your thoughts and lose touch with what's going on in the world around you.

This mindful action is to imagine your life as if it is a television series with many seasons. You are the producer, director, content creator and main character. Plan to make your next season the best ever, with ratings off the chart! To achieve this, you may need to make some changes from the last season. This time around, make your role joyful and full of purpose!

What is your purpose you say? Take some time and focus on your dream, your values and your connection. Be mindfully aware of your silent observer and the presence of divine intelligence. Simply ask "What is my purpose?" and "What is my role in the bigger picture?" Be silent and listen. Be aware of heart messages and your sense of knowing.

We live in a world where creativity is honoured and inventiveness is rewarded. Learn to connect and take action. Then connect and take action again and again. It is the mindful way to manifest what you need from moment to moment. It is also the mindful way to create a rewarding and successful season.

Make your lead character a copy of your authentic self. By creating the content for your own season, you also become a co-creator for the higher good in the world around you.

All it takes is a change in perspective to start living a life of purpose. Moreover, it is living a life of purpose that leads to living the life of your dreams. *Be Mindful!*

AWAKE

This mindful action is to practise being awake. It is almost like the final step in your mindful journey to enlightenment. When you are fully awake, you will know. If you need to ask, you're not there yet. (That reminds me of the kids in the back seat on a long trip saying "Are we there yet?")

Carl Jung said, "Your vision will become clear only when you look into your heart ... Who looks outside, dreams. Who looks inside, awakens."

Along the mindful way, you have looked inside and practised being open minded and have heart-tested your beliefs. You have become mindfully aware that you are not your thoughts. You understand the concept of the silent observer and your connection with divine intelligence.

Jon Kabat-Zinn said, "The best way to capture moments is to pay attention. This is how we cultivate mindfulness. Mindfulness means being awake. It means knowing what you are doing."

Along the mindful way, you have payed mindful attention to your thoughts without judgement. You have been curious about where your thoughts come from, made room for them or simply let them go.

The mindful way starts with mindful awareness and slowly progresses to being awake with mindfulness. Here's a couple of things to try that work for me.

The first is mindfully walking in a busy shopping centre. I let my thoughts flow and pay close attention to people, especially their gestures and body language. It never fails to amuse and amaze as mind and movement come into alignment.

The second is mindfully driving my car. I read number plates with curiosity and creativity. I am always amused and amazed at what comes to mind. I find it a great way to receive messages from source. Try it! You'll look forward to getting out and about.

Dale Carnegie said, "Today is life - the only life you are sure of. Make the most of today. Get interested in something. Shake yourself awake. Develop a hobby. Let the winds of enthusiasm sweep through you. Live today with gusto." *Be Mindful!*

PEACE & HOPE

Buddha said, "Peace comes from within. Do not seek it without."

Peace does not mean to be in a place where there is no noise, trouble or hard work. It means to be in the midst of those things and still be calm in your heart. Only you have the power to create peace in your life.

When you do find yourself in the midst of chaos, use your key thought *Be Mindful!* I realise that I keep reminding you of this mindful action. The reason is to help you cement it into your psyche. Try it when you are under pressure to perform or under pressure to make a decision. It is the absolute stress reliever.

The power of the thought *Be Mindful* is in the action of pausing your mind and becoming acutely aware. Focus on sight and sound. Have a slow look around you and use your silent observer to listen to everything in that moment.

For example, there may be multiple conversations going on. As you quieten your mind, notice how your silent observer can almost hear everything at once. Slow down and allow a sense of peace and control to come over you. Practice is always the key.

Thich Nhat Hanh said, "Peace is present right here and now, in ourselves and in everything we do and see. Every breath we take, every step we take, can be filled with peace, joy, and serenity. The question is whether or not we are in touch with it. We need only to be awake, alive in the present moment."

Nobody is going to erase all your troubles or take the load off your mind. Nobody is going to stop the constant stream of mind chatter. It is entirely up to you. It is the process of mindful observation of your thoughts that will ultimately give you peace. It is getting into the habit of noticing and letting go, noticing and letting go. Go with the flow!

Thich Nhat Hanh also said, "Hope is important because it can make the present moment less difficult to bear. If we believe that tomorrow will be better, we can bear a hardship today."

Ralph Waldo Emerson said, "Finish each day and be done with it. You have done what you could; some blunders and absurdities have crept in; forget them as soon as you can. Tomorrow is a new day; you shall begin it serenely and with too high a spirit to be encumbered with your old nonsense."

In my darkest times, when suicide seemed like the only option, there was always a glimmer of hope. There was a tiny voice that came from the depths of my soul and whispered "You will get through this". It kept me going. Stepping from the darkness into the light was a slow process for me. But it doesn't have to be for you! *Be Mindful* - and Practise, practise, practise!

Love & Kindness

Jesus of Nazereth said, "Love your neighbour as yourself"

This mindful action is to do some little thing every day to be kind. Be kind to people and make it a habit to say *thank you*. Express your appreciation with sincerity and without any expectation of something in return. When you mindfully appreciate those around you, you'll soon find more around you. When you mindfully appreciate life, you'll find that you have more life.

Be kind to your peers, your workmates and people you come into contact with throughout your day. Be kind to strangers; go one step further and be generous. Everything starts with giving. Be kind to receive kindness. Give respect to get respect. Be loving to be loved. Above all, be kind and compassionate to yourself.

Alan Cohen said, "To love yourself right now, just as you are, is to give yourself heaven. Don't wait until you die. If you wait, you die now. If you love, you live now."

The mindful action of loving yourself enables you to love another. By fully accepting and being your authentic loving self, your simple presence can make others feel really good about themselves.

Thich Nhat Hanh said, "The most precious gift we can offer others is our presence. When mindfulness embraces those we love, they will bloom like flowers."

The mindful way to change a loved one, is to change yourself. A story comes to mind. A man came to me many years ago and said "John, my marriage is on the rocks. When I first got married, everything was beautiful, we were in love. But now, we don't make love anymore and we fight almost every day".

"Do you love her?" I asked. "Yes!" He said "Very much!" I asked him to tell me about a typical day. He told me how he gets up, goes off to work and comes home in the afternoon. He explained how his wife doesn't work and how he always comes home to a messy house. He would ask "What have you been doing all day?" and then a fight would usually start.

"Try this for the next week" I said "Make your wife a cup of tea in the morning and tell her you love her. When you get home from work, say "It doesn't matter about the mess. I love you, that's what matters".

A few years later he spotted me at a local market and told me how his life had changed. In no time at all and without asking, he was coming home to a neat house and love had returned. He beamed as he also told me about their two children and blissful marriage. I love feedback like that!

The story you tell yourself is the life you create for yourself. When you tell yourself stories, make sure you tell yourself how good you are rather than how hopeless you are. Tell yourself love stories and you will create a life full of love. *Be Mindful* - and Loving!

RELATIONSHIP

This mindful action is threefold. First, it is to enrich the relationship with yourself. Second and at the same time, enrich your relationship with the Divine. Third, enrich your relationships with everyone in your circles.

There is a sanctuary within yourself, where you can retreat anytime. It is the place where your silent observer takes over from your mind. It is the place of silence and serenity where love, peace and wisdom are found. The relationship with self does not happen automatically, it requires ongoing perseverance.

The mindful way to build your own relationship is with self talk. Have a good look at yourself in the mirror and see what comes to mind. It is a great way to test how your relationship is coming along. Declare war on negativity. Expect a few battles to take place in your mind along the way. Just hang in there and keep going. You will know when victory comes.

The mindful way to communicate with the Divine is to simply talk in your mind. Start first thing in the morning and say "What are we doing today [......]?' Fill in the dots with whatever you call the Divine. Continue to talk throughout your day with mindful awareness. Don't expect to always receive answers at first, but be sure to pause your mind just in case.

This is a very personal relationship that develops over time. It is a very empowering practice that requires strong belief and trust in the connection. Be open to receive in a variety of ways. There is a reason for everything and there are no coincidences.

Make relationship with others one on one. Never let anyone else affect your relationships. This is especially applicable with family. Be mindful when people start talking about others. It is good practice to politely ask them to stop. Gently point out that you prefer to keep your relationships one on one. It is a matter of integrity.

As you enrich the relationship with yourself and the Divine, you will reflect that change and others will be drawn to you. You don't see lighthouses running around telling the world about their light. They just stand their ground and shine. *Be Mindful* - and Be the Light!

ONE LOVE

My vision for the world is One Love. When I first joined facebook back in 2008, I got to the part that said 'religion', thought for a moment and typed "We are All One, One with Spirit, One with Life!"

The beauty of my religion is that it is not a religion at all. It is an ideal, a mindset for living without limiting beliefs. It does not matter what religion you follow or whether you even follow a religion at all, you can still mindfully practice; Being One with All, Being One with Spirit, Being One with Life!

Being 'One with All' is about mindful awareness, it comes with the realisation that we are all connected. It explains how, when you first meet someone, you get intuitive feelings from 'a bit suss' to 'this person is okay'. Sometimes you don't want to know them at all, other times it is like you have known them for a lifetime.

Being 'One with Spirit' is about mindful connection. When you mindfully walk and talk with Spirit, you become aware of things happening. You come to realise and feel the power of 'One Love' when doors open or close, the phone rings or simple suggestions lead to amazing happenings. All for one love and one love for all!

Being 'One with Life' is about mindful actions, especially when you get Spiritual prompts. A Spiritual prompt is the strong feeling you get to take action. Prompts can happen at any time, any place and in almost any situation. When they come, have no fear and act without hesitation. Just do it!

I have been acting on my Spiritual prompts for many years now and I am constantly amazed at the things that happen. Many times there is no reason or logic in following prompts - at the time. But then, down the track a bit, the reason becomes apparent.

Don't take my word for it. Put it to the test. Take the thing that is on your heart and put it out there in the universe. Divine intelligence knows what is on your heart and is waiting for you to act. Synchronicity will take over and you will be on your mindful way. All that has happened to you so far, are the lessons you needed to fulfil your purpose.

When you live in the present moment, you become open to One love. One love allows you to see the beauty in everything, especially yourself. You may think of yourself as only One out of seven billion people on the planet, a mere drop in the ocean. Think of One love as that ocean; you may be only One drop but you are still part of the ocean! *Be Mindful!* - you are One Love!

INSPIRE

Inspire is a great word. Here are various dictionary meanings:

- To affect, guide, or arouse by divine influence.
- To fill with enlivening or exalting emotion
- To stimulate to action; motivate.
- To affect or touch.
- To draw forth; elicit or arouse.
- To be the cause or source of; bring about.
- To draw in air by inhaling.
- To breathe life into.
- To stimulate energies, ideals, or reverence.

The historical meaning of inspire is 'to communicate with spirit' or 'in spirit'. Here is a timeline of the inspirational people whose quotes have appeared in Mindful Actions.

- Lao Tzu [604BC-531BC]
- Buddha [563BC-483BC]
- Aristotle [384BC-322BC]
- Jesus of Nazareth [3BC-33AD]

- Ralph Waldo Emerson [1803-1882]
- Abraham Lincoln [1809-1865]
- Henry David Thoreau [1817-1862]
- Mark Twain [1835-1910]
- Mahatma Gandhi [1869-1948]
- Carl Jung [1875-1961]
- Albert Einstein [1879-1955]
- Dale Carnegie [1888-1955]
- Groucho Marx [1890-1977]
- James Thurber [1894-1961]
- Ajahn Chah [1918-1992]
- Thích Nhat Hanh [1926-]
- Dr Martin Luther King Jnr [1929-1968]
- Ram Dass [1931-]
- Osho [1931-1990]
- Dalai Lama [1935-]
- Dr. Wayne W Dyer [1940-]
- Jimi Hendrix [1942-1970]
- Diana Ross [1944-]
- Jon Kabat-Zinn [1944-]
- Paulo Coelho [1947-]
- Eckhart Tolle [1948-]
- Alan Cohen [1954-]

All through history there have been spirit filled people with a message. You are one of them! Your final mindful action is to tell your story and be an inspiration to at least one person.

My friend followed his spiritual prompt back in 1997 and told me his story. He has no idea what he did that day. There is a very good chance that he saved my life. It is a certainty that he kick-started my transformation.

The only way to transform the world is one person at a time. Start with yourself! Practise these Mindful Actions - then create your own! *Be Mindful* - and Tell Your Story!

I will finish with another great message from Ted Murray:

"Never has the possibility of personal transformation been so rapid or so urgent. The world is changing so quickly, that if we don't transform our thoughts and actions by clearing out old programming and consciously choosing to take full responsibility for living our true purpose, then life may become overwhelming. We know that we will face unprecedented challenges, but if we have transformed our attitude and our physical body to be consistently connected with pure source energy we will actually thrive and grow with the increasing challenges.

Where do you begin the transformation process? The key is to balance the process on all three levels simultaneously, the body, mind, and spirit. All reinforce each other, and when you focus too much on only one the process is held back by lack of balance. At the heart of any transformation is to get in touch with your emotions and allow them to be expressed in a non-judgmental way without attaching any stories or lasting importance to them. When you allow yourself to experience the emotions in your body, free your mind from its past programming, and consistently connect with pure source energy, then transformation can be fast, powerful and permanent."

Stay Positive
Stay Present
Stay Strong
Stay Smiling
Be Mindful!

One Love, Peace & Blessings Always!
Mindfully Yours ~ John Shearer

bemindful@outlook.com.au
www.facebook.com/mindful99
www.mindfulnesscoach.com.au
Mindfulness Coach - ABN 4217 3070 953

Special Thanks to:

Dr Russ Harris - www.actmindfully.com.au
                    - www.thehappinesstrap.com

Ted Murray - www.tennisfromtheheart.com

And especially my wife Maureen Shearer
for her great photos, help and inspiration.

Made in the USA
Lexington, KY
13 December 2014